DIS

SADDLEBACK
EDUCATIONAL PUBLISHING

DISASTERS

SADDLEBACK
EDUCATIONAL PUBLISHING
www.sdlback.com

ISBN-13: 978-1-61651-934-6
ISBN-10: 1-61651-934-7
eBook: 978-1-61247-630-8

Printed in Guangzhou, China
NOR/1114/CA21401723

18 17 16 15 14   2 3 4 5 6

CONTENTS

DATAFILE

Timeline

April 12, 1961

Yuri Gagarin, Russian cosmonaut, is the first person to enter outer space.

July 20, 1969

Neil Armstrong is the first person to walk on the moon.

Where is Russia?

Did You Know?

The *International Space Station* is the largest scientific project in world history. Astronauts from different nations work together in teams of three for months at a time.

Key Terms

astronaut—a person who is trained to go into outer space

cosmonaut—a Russian astronaut

gravity—the force that pulls objects toward the center of Earth

space station—a spacecraft that stays in space for a long time

CHAPTER 1 | Introduction

On July 20, 1969, astronaut Neil Armstrong stepped onto the moon. Millions of people watched this amazing event on television.

No one had ever stood on the moon before. It changed how people thought about our planet and the universe.

Now, space travel doesn't seem so extraordinary. A rocket blasting off isn't always big news anymore. Hundreds of astronauts and scientists have traveled in space.

Some people have even become space tourists. They pay a lot of money to spend a week in space. Now, people even live in space for months at a time.

Apollo 11 astronaut Buzz Aldrin poses for a portrait on the moon.

Science Fiction/Science Fact

It's hard to believe that less than 50 years ago, space travel was just a fantasy. Science fiction books and movies put people in outer space. But it wasn't until 1961 that someone traveled into space.

Footprint on the surface of the moon

The first person to go into space was a Russian man named Yuri Gagarin. He orbited Earth once in a Russian rocket. Then he landed safely.

Not every space mission has gone so well. Some space accidents damage very expensive equipment. Even a minor accident can cost millions of dollars. This can be a disaster for a country's space program.

Space travel is risky. Some astronauts have died in space accidents. The total number of space-related deaths is low. But these tragedies seem much bigger. Fortunately, there are very few space disasters.

The First Space Stations

The first space stations were small laboratories that orbited Earth. Astronauts traveled to the space station in rockets. They lived and worked in space for months at a time.

There is no gravity in space. People and things are weightless. Scientists studied the effects of living in space on people and other living things. They learned a lot from experiments on these early space stations.

The Russians built the first space station. *Salyut 1* was launched on April 19, 1971. The American space station, *Skylab*, was launched two years later, in May 1973.

The Russians launched their eighth space station, *Mir*, in February 1986. *Mir* means "peace" in Russian. Mir cosmonauts became the first people to spend more than a year in space.

There were many problems with the early space stations. Some of these turned into disasters. But the lessons learned from these catastrophes helped make the newest space station—the *International Space Station*—better and safer.

The *International Space Station*

Americans and Russians work with astronauts and scientists from other countries on the *International Space Station*. They do many different scientific experiments. The results of these experiments can help us learn more about life in space and life on Earth.

The *International Space Station* (ISS) orbits the Earth. Astronauts live and work on the ISS for about three to six months. Then a new crew comes to the ISS to continue the work.

The ISS is the only space station orbiting Earth. The earlier space stations are no longer in orbit.

Skylab in Trouble!

Skylab was launched on May 14, 1973. It was more than three times larger than *Salyut 1* and weighed about 100 tons. But only one minute after taking off, *Skylab* was in serious trouble. A big meteor shield fell off. It tore away a large screen of solar panels. NASA launched a team of three astronauts to fix the space station. The astronauts fixed the problem while *Skylab* orbited Earth.

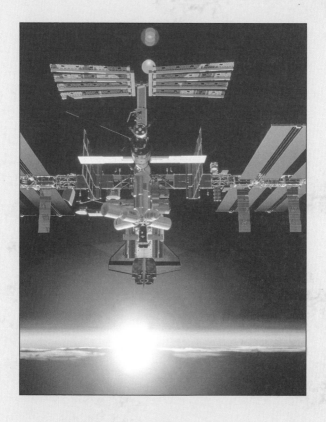

In the *International Space Station*, there are two crew cabins. Each cabin is large enough for one astronaut to sleep in.

DATAFILE

Timeline

December 3, 1967

The first successful heart transplant is performed.

January 27, 1967

A fire breaks out in the command module during practice for the *Apollo 1* mission into space.

Where is the NASA launch pad?

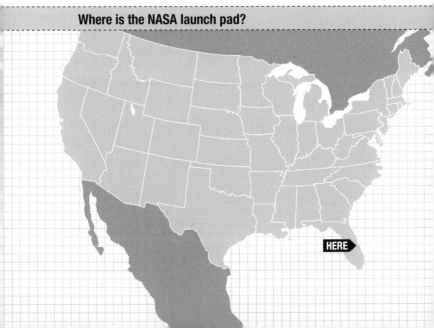

HERE

Did You Know?

In 1965, Ed White became the first American to perform the "spacewalk." He floated outside the spacecraft for 23 minutes.

Key Terms

command module—the place where the astronauts control the spaceship

National Aeronautics and Space Administration (NASA)—an organization whose mission is to plan space activities

Soviet Union—a federation of socialist republics, including Russia, that existed from 1922 to 1991

CHAPTER 2 | *Apollo 1,* 1967

The United States and the Soviet Union had space programs in the 1960s. Now both countries work together on the *International Space Station.* But, in the 1960s, they did not work together. They competed against each other. Each country wanted to be the first to rule space.

At first, the Russians were ahead in the race to space. The first person in space was Russian cosmonaut Yuri Gagarin. The United States had to catch up to the Soviet Union before they could take the lead in the space race.

The Birth of NASA

American President John F. Kennedy wanted the first person on the moon to be an American. The

National Aeronautics and Space Administration (NASA) was created in July 1958.

Its official mission was to plan and conduct space activities. Its real goal was to land American astronauts on the moon and return them safely to Earth.

The first two NASA projects were named Mercury and Gemini. The Mercury and Gemini projects put Americans into outer space. The third project, named Apollo, would land them on the moon.

The first Apollo spaceship was scheduled to take off on February 21, 1967. Thousands of people at NASA were working very hard to make that happen. It was supposed to be a great moment. Instead, the Apollo program began with tragedy.

A Fateful Test

On January 27, 1967, the *Apollo 1* crew was practicing for their trip into space. The crew consisted of Gus Grissom, Ed White, and Roger Chaffee. Grissom and White had both been into space before. *Apollo 1* was Chaffee's first mission in space.

The three astronauts were inside the command module of the spaceship. The command module is like the cockpit of a plane. It's where the astronauts sit to control the spaceship.

They were testing the plan for liftoff. The astronauts were strapped into their seats. The command module was locked and sealed.

The astronauts could talk to the NASA team using a communications system. But the system was not working properly. NASA technicians outside the command module were trying to fix that. Everything else seemed fine.

No Escape

Then, suddenly, a fire broke out inside the command module. The astronauts reported the emergency. One of them tried to open the hatch to the outside. That was the only way to escape. But the hatch was stuck. The astronauts were trapped inside!

The flames spread quickly. The fire burned the walls of the command module. Poisonous smoke filled the inside of the command module. The fire was so hot, the command module cracked. That made a very loud noise. It sounded like an explosion.

Technicians grabbed fire extinguishers. They tried to put out the fire. But smoke from the fire made it difficult to breathe. Some of them found gas masks.

Others tried to help without gas masks. It was very difficult. There was so much smoke, they could not see. They had to open the hatches using only their sense of touch.

There were three hatches on the command module. It took almost five minutes to open them all. By then, the three astronauts were dead.

No one knows exactly when or how they died. They probably died quickly from breathing poisonous smoke. Or they might have burned to death.

The heat inside the command module was very intense. It had melted their space suits. The fire had also melted the nylon from the seats. At first, no one could move the dead bodies. They were stuck to the seats.

The Investigation

The *Apollo 1* fire was a disaster for NASA. Plans for the *Apollo 1* launch were put on hold.

There was an investigation. But the cause of the fire was never discovered. The most likely explanation was that a spark from bad electrical wiring started the fire.

The spark ignited oxygen gas inside the command module. There was a very high level of oxygen inside the command module. Oxygen burns quickly.

The tragedy was also the result of poor planning and design. Many safety changes were made following the *Apollo 1* disaster. A new fast-release escape hatch was put in the command module. The new hatch could be opened from inside in seven seconds.

The Apollo program was delayed by 21 months. But it did recover after the tragic fire. *Apollo 11* astronauts Neil Armstrong and Buzz Aldrin were the first people to walk on the moon. Five other Apollo missions also put people on the surface of the moon.

The late President Kennedy's wish was realized. And despite its tragic beginning, the Apollo program was a tremendous success.

Apollo 1 astronauts (L-R), Virgil "Gus" Grissom, Edward White, and Roger Chaffee, suited up at the Saturn launch pad. A few days later, all three would be killed in an electrical fire in the command module during testing.

DATAFILE

Timeline

April 11, 1970

Apollo 13 lifts off on a mission to the moon.

April 13, 1970

There is an explosion on the *Apollo 13*.

Where is the Pacific Ocean?

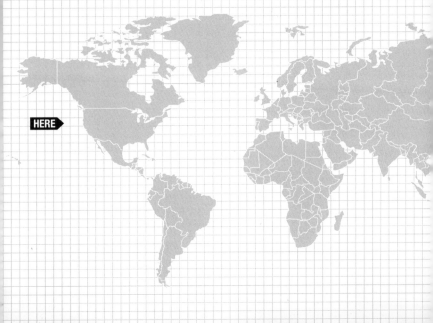

Key Terms

German measles—a disease that causes the neck to become swollen and the skin to develop red spots

lunar module—a separate structure designed to land the astronauts on the moon

CHAPTER 3 | *Apollo 13,* 1970

The *Apollo 11* astronauts were the first people to walk on the moon. Millions of people knew the names Neil Armstrong and Buzz Aldrin.

Apollo 12 astronauts also landed on the moon. *Apollo 13* was going to be the third time American astronauts walked on the moon.

But *Apollo 13* never landed on the moon. Two days after it took off from Earth, *Apollo 13* was in trouble. A tank of oxygen exploded.

The blast damaged the spacecraft. It looked as though the astronauts would not be able to return to Earth. They might be stranded in space!

Unlucky 13?

Some people believe the number 13 is unlucky. The explosion on *Apollo 13* happened on the 13th of April. But the mission's bad luck began even before the spacecraft took off.

Three days before launch, there was a last-minute crew change. The *Apollo 13* crew was accidentally exposed to German measles.

Two of the crew had already had the disease. They could not get it again. But the command module pilot had never had German measles.

NASA doctors were afraid he would get sick during the mission. They would not let him go on the mission. The back-up pilot, Jack Swigert, replaced him.

Swigert was an experienced pilot. But he had not been training with the other two crew members. Space missions depend on excellent teamwork. The three astronauts had to learn how to work together. And they had only two days to get used to each other.

Three...two...one...liftoff!

Apollo 13 lifted off on April 11, 1970. At first everything went well. All systems were working properly.

On their third day in space, the astronauts made a TV broadcast. They showed how they lived and worked in space. People back on Earth could see what it was like to be weightless.

But less than ten minutes after they finished this, something went very wrong.

There was a sharp bang. The spaceship shook. Warning lights in the command module showed that two of the three fuel supplies were gone. The fuel provided electricity for everything on the spacecraft.

The astronauts quickly realized they would not be able to land on the moon. There wasn't enough power left. They were terribly disappointed.

Then they saw that their oxygen supplies were dangerously low. One of the astronauts looked out the window. He saw the oxygen gas spraying out of the spacecraft.

This was much more serious than not landing on the moon. They needed this oxygen to breathe. Without it, they would die. And without power, the spacecraft would not be able to get them home.

The three astronauts realized that making it back to Earth alive would be a miracle.

No Air, No Water, No Power

The astronauts lost most of their oxygen within three hours. They also lost their water.

There was almost no power left. The command module was supposed to be the astronaut's control center in space. Now it was useless.

But the lunar module was still attached. This was the astronauts' only hope. They moved into the lunar module. It became their lifeboat in space.

Lunar Module Lifeboat

The lunar module had its own supply of oxygen. It also had a separate power supply.

The explosion had not affected the lunar module. It still had oxygen and power. But would it be enough to keep the astronauts alive till they could return safely to Earth?

The lunar module was designed to land two astronauts on the moon. After two days on the moon, the two astronauts would return to the command module. The third astronaut would remain in the command module.

Now all three astronauts needed to live in the lunar module. It would take them four days to get back to Earth.

The lunar module was not designed to support three astronauts for four days. Still, it was the only way the astronauts could survive their trip back to Earth. They had to make it work.

Struggle for Survival

The astronauts had enough oxygen to breathe. They circled the moon. Then they used the power left in the lunar module to push themselves back toward Earth.

They were on their way home. But there was very little water. Each astronaut drank less than a cup of water a day. That was less than a fifth of what they were supposed to drink.

There was no power to heat the spacecraft. The astronauts were freezing cold.

There was no hot water to put in their food either. Space food is usually dehydrated. Normally the astronauts would add hot water to the food, then eat it. But without hot water, the food was useless. The astronauts ate very little.

It was a long, cold, hungry four days. But the astronauts returned safely to Earth on April 17. They splashed down into the Pacific Ocean. They were tired, hungry, and thirsty. One of the astronauts had lost 14 pounds. But they were alive, and very happy to be home.

A Successful Failure?

The *Apollo 13* mission did not land on the moon. It was a $375 million failure. But everyone was very relieved the three astronauts were safe. Getting them home alive under the circumstances was a tremendous achievement.

Navy swimmers fasten a floatation collar around the *Apollo 13* capsule as it floats after splashdown in the Pacific Ocean.

Left to right: Fred Haise, lunar module pilot; James Lovell, commander; and Jack Swigert, command module pilot, wave to a crowd after their successful splashdown.

DATAFILE

Timeline

April 19, 1971

Salyut 1, the world's first space station, is launched.

April 23, 1971

The first space station crew leaves for *Salyut 1*.

Where was the Soviet Union?

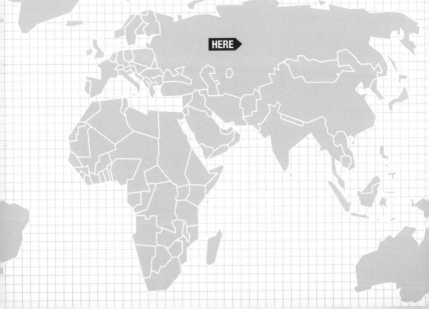

Did You Know?

Vladimir M. Komarov was the first person to die in a space mission, in 1967. While returning to Earth, the main parachute did not open. The rocket crashed into the ground.

Key Terms

space suit—a special suit that allows astronauts to survive in space

suffocate—to stop a person from breathing

valve—a device that controls the flow of a gas

CHAPTER 4 | *Soyuz 11,* 1971

The Russians knew they could not win the moon race. Instead, they focused on building the first space station. They launched *Salyut 1* in April 1971.

Salyut 1 was the world's first space station. *Salyut* means "salute" in Russian. The name was chosen in memory of cosmonaut Yuri Gagarin. Gagarin was the first person in space. He was a Russian hero. In 1968, Gagarin was killed in a plane crash.

Soyuz

The *Salyut 1* space station was launched without anyone inside. Cosmonauts traveled to the space station on a small rocket ship called *Soyuz.*

Soyuz means "union" in Russian. These rockets could make one trip up into space and back. A new *Soyuz* rocket was used for each trip.

The first crew arrived at *Salyut 1* four days after the space station was launched. But they did not get inside. They could not open the hatch. They came back to Earth without entering the space station.

The second crew did get into the space station. This was the first time a space station was occupied. The three cosmonauts stayed on *Salyut 1* for 23 days. That was the longest anyone had ever been in space. The Russians were very proud of this achievement.

Space Science

Space stations are like small laboratories. The cosmonauts did experiments. They wanted to see how people reacted to being in space for long periods of time.

They studied themselves to find out how their bodies reacted to being weightless. They also studied Earth's weather. The information they gathered would help improve weather forecasts.

The cosmonauts completed their experiments. It was time for them to leave the space station. They boarded their *Soyuz* rocket.

The rocket separated from the space station. It orbited Earth three times. The cosmonauts were ready to come back to Earth.

It seemed like their mission was a complete success. But disaster was about to strike. The three men would not make it back to Earth alive.

Dead on Arrival

Mission Control tried to contact the cosmonauts as they returned to Earth. But there was no answer. Still, everything seemed all right.

Soyuz rockets were programmed to return to Earth. The crew did not have to pilot the rocket back to Earth.

The *Soyuz 11* landed on schedule. The ground crew opened the hatch. They were ready to welcome the three heroes home.

But instead they had a horrible shock. The three men were dead. They had died in space.

At first, these deaths were a mystery. No one knew what had happened. The cosmonauts were found still strapped in their seats. There were no signs that they had tried to get out.

One idea was that they had all suffered heart attacks. But that was not what happened. The tragedy was caused by a fault in the rocket.

A valve opened by accident. The air inside the rocket rushed out. The three men suffocated to death.

If they had been wearing space suits, they would have survived. But the *Soyuz 11* was very small. The three cosmonauts were squeezed inside.

There was not enough room for them to wear space suits. They relied on air inside the rocket to breathe. But when the valve opened, all the air escaped. They could not breathe, so they died.

This disaster delayed the Soviet space program. The Soviet Union did not send a new crew to *Salyut 1*. Two years passed before they sent any more cosmonauts into space. And from then on, all cosmonauts wore spacesuits for launch and landing.

Launch of a *Soyuz* mission, June 24, 1982

CHAPTER 5 | *Challenger*, 1986

DATAFILE

Timeline

April 12, 1981

The first space shuttle, *Columbia*, is launched.

January 28, 1986

The *Challenger* space shuttle explodes less than two minutes after liftoff.

Where is New Hampshire?

HERE

Key Terms

ground—to stop

seal—a cap placed over the lid of a container

space shuttle—a reusable spacecraft that lifts off like a rocket and lands like an airplane

Teacher in Space Program (TISP)—a NASA program designed to give teachers a chance to go into space

CHAPTER 5 | *Challenger,* 1986

The American space shuttle takes off like a rocket. It orbits the Earth like a spacecraft. And it lands like an airplane.

NASA started the space shuttle program in the 1970s. They wanted a spacecraft that could carry heavy loads into space. They also wanted this new spacecraft to be reusable.

Previous spacecraft could be used only once. These early American and Russian rockets could make only one trip into space and back.

The same space shuttle can be used again and again. It can also carry very large, heavy objects. It brings satellites and parts of the *International Space Station* up into space to orbit Earth.

The first space shuttle, *Columbia*, lifted off on April 12, 1981. Since then, there have been more than a hundred successful space shuttle missions. But the most famous space shuttle mission was a disaster.

Space Shuttle *Challenger*

Challenger was NASA's second space shuttle. It started flying in 1982. It successfully completed nine missions.

Challenger's tenth mission was the 25th space shuttle flight. *Challenger* was originally scheduled to lift off January 22, 1986. But there were many delays.

Bad weather and strong winds were partly to blame. There were also problems with the space shuttle itself. Part of the hatch had to be sawed off when it could not be removed any other way. There were other problems, too. One of the fire monitors was not working properly.

Finally, almost a week late, *Challenger* lifted off. But its flight would last less than two minutes and end in tragedy.

A Teacher in Space

Usually only NASA astronauts and scientists go up on the space shuttle. But the tenth *Challenger* mission was special. It was the first flight of a new NASA program called the Teacher in Space Program (TISP).

The *Challenger* was scheduled to carry Sharon Christa McAuliffe, the first teacher to fly in space. Christa McAuliffe was a high school teacher from New Hampshire. She was going to teach lessons from space to students around the country.

More than 11,000 teachers applied to TISP. They all wanted to go up on the space shuttle. McAuliffe trained for many months before the flight.

She was very excited about the opportunity to be part of the space program. Her students were very proud of their teacher.

The liftoff was broadcast live. TVs were turned on in schools all over the country so children could watch the *Challenger* lift off as it happened. They watched the *Challenger* lift off. And they saw it destroyed in a puff of smoke.

Challenger blew apart 73 seconds after it took off. The space shuttle and its seven-person crew were lost.

Millions of people watched this disaster as it happened on television. It was a horrible shock. It left America, and the world, stunned and sad.

A Terrible Loss

NASA had never lost an astronaut in flight. Now it lost an entire seven-person crew.

The entire space shuttle program was grounded. NASA had to figure out what went wrong. They needed to make sure the same thing wouldn't happen to the other space shuttles.

Space shuttle *Challenger* exploding in flight

They looked closely at pictures of the *Challenger* blasting off. There was a puff of smoke coming from one of the rocket boosters less than a second after take off.

Computer images confirmed there was a problem with one of the solid rocket booster seals. Hot gas leaked out. This started a fire. The fire caused the fuel to explode within the rocket, which destroyed the space shuttle.

New Safety Plans

NASA made many changes after the *Challenger* disaster. They fixed the seals in the other space shuttles. New, stricter safety plans were put into effect.

NASA built a new space shuttle in 1991. The Endeavour replaced *Challenger*. Once again, NASA had a fleet of four space shuttles.

DATAFILE

Timeline

February 1, 2003

Columbia explodes as it returns to Earth.

April 16, 2003

Columbia Space Shuttle Program Director, Ron Dittemore, decides to leave his job. He was director for 26 years.

Where is Texas?

HERE

Key Terms

bail out—to escape

experiment—a scientific test

parachute—a piece of material that opens like an umbrella to give a person a safe landing

CHAPTER 6 | *Columbia,* 2003

The second shuttle disaster happened in February 2003. Space shuttle *Columbia* blew apart as it was returning to Earth.

The Crew

Seven astronauts were on board *Columbia* when it exploded. Six were Americans. Rick Husband was the commander. William McCool was the pilot. The other American astronauts were Kalpana Chawla, Michael Anderson, David Brown, and Laurel Clark. The seventh astronaut was from Israel. His name was Ilan Ramon. Ramon was a colonel in the Israeli Air Force. This was the first time an Israeli astronaut had gone into space.

Only three of the *Columbia* astronauts had been in space before. It was the first trip for Brown, Clark, McCool , and Ramon.

Astronauts wear special suits when they return to Earth. These suits have a parachute. But *Columbia* blew apart so quickly there was no time for the crew to bail out.

Small Holes, Big Trouble

This disaster happened just 16 minutes before *Columbia* was supposed to land. The outside of the space shuttle gets very, very hot as it comes down to Earth. Special tiles protect the space shuttle and the astronauts from this heat. But this time, something went wrong. Super hot gas got inside the left wing of the shuttle. This caused the shuttle to blow apart.

NASA wanted to know what caused these small holes. There were several possibilities. During lift-off, a piece of foam broke off and hit the wing. This may have damaged tiles that protect the shuttle when it comes back to Earth. Or maybe something else hit the shuttle and made a hole.

Columbia's 28th Mission

The *Columbia* astronauts were almost home when their mission turned to tragedy. They had been in space for 16 days. Some astronauts are also scientists. Their job is to complete experiments in space. Many of these focus on how the human body reacts to being in space. On this mission, astronauts were studying why people lose bone and muscle when they stay in space.

They also studied spiders. Students in Australia had prepared that experiment. They were testing whether spiders can spin webs in zero gravity.

Picking up the Pieces

Some people on the ground heard a loud boom when the *Columbia* exploded. They saw pieces of the space shuttle fall to the ground. Luckily, no one was hurt by the falling pieces.

Pieces from the space shuttle were scattered over a very large area. Thousands of police, soldiers, and volunteers collected as many as they could find. NASA hopes that studying what's left of the shuttle will help them answer more questions about what happened.

The crew of the space shuttle *Columbia* walk onto the launch pad. In the first row, pilot William McCool (left) and commander Rick Husband (right). In the second row are mission specialists Kalpana Chawla (left) and Laurel Clark (right). In the last row, payload specialist Ilan Ramon, payload commander Michael Anderson and mission specialist David Brown. Ilan Ramon was the first Israeli astronaut to travel into space.

Columbia was the first space shuttle. Its first trip into space was in 1981. Here the shuttle *Columbia* lifts off for its last mission on January 16, 2003. The *Columbia* was lost when it broke up upon re-entry to Earth on February 1, 2003. The disaster happened at the end of *Columbia*'s 28th trip.

DATAFILE

Timeline

September 24, 2011

The Upper Atmosphere Research Satellite falls to earth and lands in the Pacific Ocean.

January 15, 2012

The 13-ton Russian space probe, *Phobos-Grunt,* crashes into the Pacific Ocean, about 700 miles off the west coast of Chile.

Where is Chile?

Did You Know?

Wilhelm Conrad Röntgen won the Nobel Prize in physics in 1901 for the discovery of x-rays. He named his discovery X-radiation. The "X" stood for the math term that means something unknown.

Key Terms

deploy—to put into use or action

plummet—to fall straight down, plunge

probe—an exploratory device

CHAPTER 7 | Falling Satellites

In 2011, more than 220,000 pounds of debris or "space junk" fell to earth. On average, one piece of space junk plummets to earth each day. It used to be that most debris came from the explosions of old launch vehicle booster rockets. Now, most space junk is the result of colliding and exploding satellites.

Since the launch of the first artificial satellite, *Sputnik 1,* on October 4, 1957, over 28,000 orbiting objects have been launched into space. Almost 1,000 are still up there. Each year, around 75 new launches are added. So space is not really empty. It can get crowded!

From late summer 2011 to January 2012, three major satellites plunged to earth. Each disabled satellite created the danger of large pieces of falling space junk.

NASA's *Upper Atmospheric Research Satellite (UARS)*

The *Upper Atmosphere Research Satellite* was deployed in 1991. It was as big as a school bus and weighed approximately six tons. The space shuttle *Discovery* launched the *UARS*. Its mission was to study the earth's atmosphere, particularly the ozone layer. The satellite ran out of fuel and was classified as a "dead satellite" in 2005.

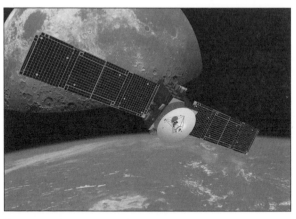

One of many thousands of satellites orbiting Earth.

NASA estimated that several thousand pounds of space junk could fall to earth. The *UARS* made an uncontrolled re-entry into the earth's atmosphere on September 24, 2011. "Uncontrolled" means the satellite has no propulsion system on board.

According to NASA, the *UARS* broke apart and landed in the Pacific Ocean. Twenty-six pieces of the satellite weighing 1,200 pounds might have survived re-entry.

NASA reported that our odds of getting hit by a piece of space junk were about 1 in 21 trillion. But the chance of someone, somewhere on the planet getting hit by pieces of the *UARS* was 1 in 3,200.

Germany's Roentgen Satellite (*ROSAT*)

Germany's *ROSAT* was a satellite X-ray telescope launched in 1990. It weighed over 4,000 pounds and was named for the Nobel Prize–winning scientist Wilhelm Röntgen. During its time in space, *ROSAT* mapped over 100,000 stars, supernovas, and cosmic rays.

The most dangerous piece of space junk from *ROSAT* was its telescope mirror. It weighed almost two tons. And it was resistant to extreme heat.

ROSAT fell to earth on Saturday, October 23, 2011. Tracking radar in Germany showed a ball of flame with a unicorn-like horn, which was also burning. *ROSAT* landed somewhere in the Bay of Bengal in the Indian Ocean. The telescope mirror has not been recovered.

Russia's *Phobos-Grunt* Probe

Phobos-Grunt launched on November 9, 2011. It was a $165 million project. The probe weighed more than 13 tons. The two-year mission of the probe was to visit Phobos, one of Mars's moons. *Phobos-Grunt* would carry out the first attempt to bring soil samples back from the tiny moon. The probe would also study dust storms and radiation on Mars.

The probe failed. The secondary booster engines did not fire. Mission control in Russia could not fix the problem. *Phobos-Grunt* never made it out of the earth's orbit.

Phobos-Grunt dropped in altitude a little each day. Since the vehicle weighed 13.5 tons, it was one of the heaviest objects to make an uncontrolled fall to earth.

On January 15, 2012, *Phobos-Grunt* crashed into the Pacific Ocean approximately 700 miles off the west coast of Chile. The Russians estimated that there were two dozen major pieces of space junk. There was no more information given to the public about what happened to *Phobos-Grunt*.

Biggest Litter Bug in the Universe

The biggest creator of space junk is Russia's *Mir* Space Station. In March, 2001, the space station began a controlled descent through the earth's atmosphere above the Pacific Ocean near Fiji.

Most of the space station burned up in the atmosphere. About 1,500 pieces of the station reached the earth's surface. Beachgoers in Fiji snapped photos of blazing bits of *Mir* debris. There were reports of sonic booms caused by heavy falling debris.

A Curtain of Debris

While getting hit in the head with a piece of space satellite sounds scary, it probably will never happen. The real problem in space is orbiting satellites hitting each other. The world depends on working satellites for most of our communications.

If we keep sending up satellites, we might create a traffic jam in space. Space junk from older satellites keeps building up. This could create a barrier around the planet. The barrier would make it dangerous to get to space.

Clear Skies

There is little chance one of us will get hit by a falling piece of space junk. We are pretty spread out on planet Earth. Humans use only about 5 percent of the planet. And 70 percent of the planet is water. National Geographic estimates that if our entire population of 7 billion stood shoulder-to-shoulder, we would all fit into the city of Los Angeles.

So you can look up for falling satellites. But you'll probably just see the sky.

CHAPTER 8 | Asteroid Impact

DATAFILE

Timeline

June 30, 1908

An asteroid falls into the earth's atmosphere and causes a tremendous explosion over Siberia. It levels trees up to ten miles away.

January 2011

The AG5 asteroid is discovered. It is approximately the size of a football field

Where is Siberia?

Did You Know?

There are more than 90,000 asteroids orbiting between Mars and Jupiter. It is thought that these asteroids never managed to fuse together as a planet because of Jupiter's gravitational pull.

Key Terms

asteroid—objects made up mostly of rock, carbon, and metal

orbital path—path of a body in a field of force surrounding another body

simulation—a mathematical model for some process or situation in order to estimate its characteristics

CHAPTER 8 | Asteroid Impact

Action movies show frightening asteroids that explode into the earth and wipe out humans. Is this really possible? Scientists believe that at some time in the future, a major asteroid will slam into the earth. This is the kind of earth-changing disaster that may have killed off dinosaurs 65 million years ago.

If an asteroid were to hit the earth, the results would be catastrophic. Researchers at the University of California at Santa Cruz conducted a computer simulation of a large asteroid strike. Computer simulations show scientists what their ideas might look like in reality.

The researchers chose the Atlantic Ocean for the asteroid's simulated impact point. The spot was located just over 350 miles from the coast of the United States. Since the earth is 70 percent water, it is likely any asteroid strike would hit the oceans.

The simulated asteroid hit the ocean at nearly 40,000 miles per hour. It blew a hole in the water 11 miles wide that reached three miles down to the ocean floor. As water rushed back into the hole, huge waves spread out in all directions.

The waves kept building in height. Two hours after impact, tsunami waves over 400 feet high destroyed large areas of the eastern United States.

What is an Asteroid?

Asteroids are objects made up mostly of rock, carbon, and metal. Think of asteroids as debris left over from the creation of the Sun, the moons, and the planets some 4.5 billion years ago. Most asteroids orbit the sun in a tightly packed area between Mars and Jupiter.

Asteroids orbiting within 250 million miles of the Sun are called Near Earth Asteroids or NEAs. NASA estimates that the earth is hit every day with basketball-sized NEAs. Several times a year, car-sized asteroids hit the earth. Asteroids can also be as small as pebbles.

Asteroids have amazing destructive power. In 1908, a small asteroid around 150 feet wide exploded in the atmosphere above Siberia. More than 500,000 acres of forest were immediately destroyed by the explosion that resulted.

Historic Asteroids

For over 200 years, Ceres was thought to be the largest asteroid. It was discovered in 1801 and is 600 miles wide. But in 2001, the KX76 asteroid was discovered. KX76 is at least 750 miles across. It is located approximately 4 billion miles from Earth.

NASA's Near Earth Object (NEO) Program Office tracks and identifies asteroids. They classify large asteroids as those bigger than half a mile wide. These asteroids hit the earth every million years or so. Larger asteroids, like the one that killed off the dinosaurs, are even rarer. They strike the earth every tens of millions of years.

Are People Really at Risk?

There is a lot of "space" in space. If all the asteroids were put together to form a planet, it would only be the size of the moon. And most of them are in an orbit around 250 million miles from the sun. The largest asteroids are millions of miles apart from one another.

The Barringer meteor crater near Winslow, Arizona. Crashing 49,000 years ago, the meteor was 150 feet across, weighed roughly 300,000 tons, and was traveling at a speed of 40,000 miles per hour.

And the earth's population is around 7 billion people. But we are very spread out. If we all came together in one place, we could fit into the city of Los Angeles. Basically, what scientists are saying is that it is hard to hit a human being with an asteroid!

But it Could Happen

In 2011, an asteroid was discovered that scientist believed posed a threat to the earth. The asteroid was named Asteroid 2011 AG5. It was nearly 500 feet across. It had the potential to hit the earth in less than 30 years.

After studying AG5, NASA discovered that the asteroid had changed its orbit. The pull of the earth's gravity probably was a factor in altering the AG5's orbital path.

The odds are extremely remote now that the AG5 asteroid will hit the earth. Scientists will continue to study AG5. In 2013, AG5 will orbit within 90 million miles of the earth. This will give astronomers a better idea if the asteroid is a future threat to the earth.

How to Stop an Asteroid?

It would be hard but not impossible to stop an asteroid from hitting the earth. Some people think we could just shoot the asteroid with a nuclear weapon. But this would just create millions more smaller asteroids!

NASA is testing several ways to stop asteroids from hitting the earth. One involves launching a space probe that would land on the asteroid. The extra weight would alter the asteroid's orbit and carry it away from the earth.

NASA is also developing a "Kinetic Interceptor." The Interceptor would launch itself into the asteroid and bump into it. It would be deflected from its path and would not hit the earth.

Humans should be thankful that asteroids exist. Asteroids are probably responsible for bringing life-giving water and carbon molecules to our planet early in its history.

Although the chance of the earth being struck by a large asteroid is extremely small, the consequences would be catastrophic. That's why we have to continue to study asteroids.

DATAFILE

Timeline

September 13, 1959

The USSR's unmanned *Luna 2* becomes the first spacecraft to land on the the moon.

July 20, 1969

Four days after launching from the Kennedy Space Center in Florida, the *Apollo 11* crew land the first manned spacecraft on the surface of the moon.

Where is Florida?

HERE

Key Terms

microbes—a minute form of life

routine—commonplace, typical, daily activity

sophisticated—lacking simplicity, complex

suborbital—flight that does not go into orbit around the earth

CHAPTER 9 | Future of Space

The future of American space exploration is up in the air. No Americans have been to the moon since *Apollo 17* in 1972. America's Space Shuttle program has been discontinued. Are Americans bored with the routine of space travel? Or is there another reason?

Space exploration is dangerous and expensive. Many scientists believe America's future in space depends on using robots. Robots will help. But only living, breathing humans can push America's space program into exciting new directions.

Space Tourism

Virgin Galactic is developing space tourism vehicles like *SpaceShipTwo*. These vehicles will carry passengers to the edge of space. All Galactic flights will be suborbital. A suborbital flight is one that does not go into orbit around the earth. But at an altitude of at least 68 miles, passengers will get to experience six minutes of weightlessness.

Virgin Galactic says it has taken deposits from more than 500 passengers. Each passenger has paid $200,000 for a ride on *SpaceShipTwo*. These flights will not be like traditional space flights. Six space tourists and two pilots will board a space vehicle that looks like an airplane. This airplane-like vehicle will be attached underneath a larger airplane.

The larger airplane will fly to an altitude of 48,000 feet. Then, *SpaceShipTwo* will disconnect from the larger plane and fire its rockets. This will boost the plane to over 340,000 feet. Once the rocket engine burns out, passengers will start to experience weightlessness. They will be able to look out of the windows and see space with the earth curving around below. The whole experience will last around two hours.

Unmanned Flights

Our future in space will depend heavily on unmanned flights. This is safer and less expensive than sending humans into space. Unmanned flights can perform all kinds of sophisticated experiments and missions. Unmanned robots and telescopes have shown us amazing pictures of many planets.

Two recently launched unmanned space missions include *Aquarius* and the *Mars Curiosity* rover. *Aquarius* launched in 2011. Its three-year mission is to study the surface of the sea. The data is used by scientists to understand how weather patterns affect the sea.

The *Mars Curiosity* rover launched in 2011. It is the most technologically advanced rover ever launched. The rover will help scientists determine whether Mars can be hospitable to microbes. Microbes are earth's smallest creatures. They are the foundation of life on earth.

Unmanned space probes are helping scientists study satellites and asteroids. Space scientists are currently tracking roughly 1,100 active satellites. They are also tracking more than 22,000 pieces of debris. Space probes can be used to destroy or alter the path of dangerous satellites and asteroids.

SpaceX – The Future is Now

On May 22, 2012, the space exploration company SpaceX worked with NASA to launch an unmanned cargo capsule named *Dragon*. It was heading to the International Space Station orbiting 240 miles above the earth. SpaceX wanted to prove that private space companies could complete routine space missions.

The SpaceX *Dragon* mission lasted nine days. It carried 1,100 pounds of equipment. Not long after launching (photo on right), SpaceX tested *Dragon*'s navigational and solar equipment. They passed these tests perfectly. But bigger tests followed.

The space station was orbiting the earth at about 17,000 miles per hour. *Dragon* slowly flew underneath the space station. It had to get close, about a mile and a half away. NASA and SpaceX tested the *Dragon*'s communications systems. Again, the systems tested perfectly.

The *Dragon* moved closer to the space station. The slightest mistake could damage the space station and harm the passengers inside. The *Dragon* circled slowly around the space station. The capsule slowed down and seemed to hang in space. It moved to within 30 feet of the space station.

The next step was the most dangerous and important part of the entire mission. A robotic arm on the space station reached for the *Dragon* capsule.

It grabbed hold of the capsule and brought it in to a docking station. It was now official. SpaceX was the first private company to successfully send a craft to the space station.

Astronauts aboard the space station spent the next week unloading the *Dragon*'s cargo. Approximately 1,400 pounds of equipment and experiments from the station were packed onto the *Dragon* for its return journey. Finally, the *Dragon* separated from the space station. It fired its rockets and headed back to earth.

The descent went smoothly. The *Dragon* glided through the earth's atmosphere and gradually slowed down. Three large parachutes attached to the capsule slowed it further. It descended to the ocean at under 12 miles per hour.

The *Dragon* dropped into the Pacific Ocean, about 600 miles from Baja, California. Just about every scientist termed the mission a spectacular success. SpaceX founder Elon Musk called the mission a "significantly historical step forward in space travel."

Working with NASA, SpaceX will begin regular unmanned supply missions to the space station. But that's not all. SpaceX plans to send humans to Mars in the next 20 years.

Glossary

astronaut—a person who is trained to go into outer space

bail out—to escape

command module—the place where the astronauts control the spaceship

cosmonaut—a Russian astronaut

experiment—a scientific test

German measles—a disease that causes the neck to become swollen and the skin to develop red spots

gravity—the force that pulls objects toward the center of Earth

ground—to stop

lunar module—a separate structure designed to land the astronauts on the moon

National Aeronautics and Space Administration (NASA)—an organization whose mission is to plan space activities

parachute—a piece of material that opens like an umbrella to give a person a safe landing

seal—a cap placed over the lid of a container

Soviet Union—a federation of socialist republics, including Russia, that existed from 1922 to 1991

space shuttle—a reusable spacecraft that lifts off like a rocket and lands like an airplane

space station—a spacecraft that stays in space for a long time

space suit—a special suit that allows astronauts to survive in space

suffocate—to stop a person from breathing

Teacher in Space Program (TISP)—a NASA program designed to give teachers a chance to go into space

valve—a device that controls the flow of a gas

Index